HORSE FARM

APPALOOSA HORSES

NorwoodHouse Press

ANNE ACCARDI

Cataloging-in-Publication Data

Names: Accardi, Anne.
Title: Appaloosa horses / Anne Accardi.
Description: Buffalo, NY : Norwood House Press, 2027. | Series: Horse farm | Includes glossary and index.
Identifiers: ISBN 9781978580800 (pbk.) | ISBN 9781978580817 (library bound) | ISBN 9781978580824 (ebook)
Subjects: LCSH: Appaloosa horse--Juvenile literature.
Classification: LCC SF293.A7 A33 2027 | DDC 636.13--dc23

Published in 2027 by
Norwood House Press
2544 Clinton Street
Buffalo, NY 14224

Designer: Rhea Magaro
Editor: Kim Thompson

Photo credits: Cover, pp. 1, 5 Rita_Kochmarjova/Shutterstock.com; p. 6 Library of Congress; p. 7 Kirk Fisher/Shutterstock.com; p. 9 mveldhuizen/Shutterstock.com; p. 10 AnetaZabranska/Shutterstock.com; p. 11 Bettina Calder/Shutterstock.com; p. 12 Georgia Evans/Shutterstock.com; p. 13 Julia Shepeleva/Shutterstock.com; p. 14 slowmotiongli/Shutterstock.com; p. 15 Tom McGinty/Shutterstock.com; p. 17 Bob Pool/Shutterstock.com; p. 18 Geri Lynn Smith/Shutterstock.com; p. 19 Olga_i/Shutterstock.com; p. 21 www.MartinaBurianova.cz/Shutterstock.com;

Printed in the United States of America

CPSIA compliance information: Batch #CSNHP27: For further information contact Norwood House Press at 1-800-237-9932.

TABLE OF CONTENTS

Meet the Appaloosa Horse.......................................4
What Do Appaloosas Look Like?..............................8
How Do Appaloosas Help People?..........................12
What Do Appaloosas Need?....................................18
Glossary..22
Thinking Questions..23
Index..24
About the Author...24

Meet the Appaloosa Horse

The Appaloosa is a popular horse **breed**. Appaloosas are also called Appys. They are known for their beautiful spots.

They were first bred by the

Nez Perce tribe.

They got their name from the Palouse River in Idaho. The Appaloosa is the state horse of Idaho.

What Do Appaloosas Look Like?

Appys come in many colors. Some have white spots that look like snow. Some have dark spots like a leopard.

Appys are strong and **muscular**.

Their **manes** and tails are thin.

Their **hooves** have stripes.

HOW DO APPALOOSAS HELP PEOPLE?

Appys have tough hooves. They are **gentle** and friendly. They are great for riding on trails.

Many kids learn to ride on them.

Appys have good **endurance**. They can go for a long time before they get tired.

They are used in races and **rodeos**.

People love to see horses with spotted **coats**. Appys are used in many movies and TV shows.

What Do Appaloosas Need?

Appys need healthy food. They eat grass, **hay**, and grains. They also drink a lot of water.

They need lots of exercise.

These horses can get sunburned. They need shade in the day. Some even need sunscreen.

Glossary

breed (breed): one type or kind of an animal

coats (kohts): hair or fur that covers animals' bodies

endurance (en-DOOR-uhns): being able to do something hard for a long time

gentle (JEN-tuhl): soft and mild; not rough

hay (hay): long grass that is cut, dried, and used as food for farm animals

hooves (hoovz): hard parts that cover the feet of horses, pigs, and other animals

manes (mayns): long growths of hair on a horse's head and neck

muscular (MUHS-kyuh-lur): having strong muscles

Nez Perce (nez purs): Native American people who originally lived on land that is now Idaho, Washington, and Oregon

rodeos (ROH-dee-ohz): contests in which cowboys and cowgirls ride horses, rope calves, and do other tricks

Thinking Questions

1. Who first bred Appaloosas?
2. How did Appaloosas get their name?
3. Describe an Appy's coat.
4. Why are Appaloosas good for riding?
5. Why are Appys used in movies and TV shows?

Index

colors 8

food 18

hooves 11, 12

Idaho 7

Nez Perce 6

personality 12, 14

riding 12, 13, 15

spots 4, 8, 16

About the Author

Anne Accardi is a librarian who loves reading books and learning new things! She lives in Kansas City, Missouri. When she's not writing, Anne enjoys listening to music, exploring nature around the city, and spending time with her family.